CAP

Contemporary A Cappella Songbook

Volume 1
Third Edition

**A Cappella Arrangements by
Anne Raugh &
Deke Sharon**

T0059103

EXCLUSIVELY DISTRIBUTED BY

HAL•LEONARD®
CORPORATION

7777 W. BLUEMOUND RD. P.O. BOX 13819 MILWAUKEE, WI 53213

TABLE OF CONTENTS

ACKNOWLEDGMENTS

This project has been over a year in the making, and during the course of that time many people have contributed to the final product. Although we can't name them all, we can at least mention some of them and hope that the rest will forgive us our brevity.

We'd like to thank John Neal and Don Gooding, founders and proprietors of the Primarily A Cappella catalog, for their support and encouragement, and for making so much a cappella music available to so many. We'd also like to thank the groups whose performances of the pieces in this collection have inspired both singers and arrangers. And we'd like to thank the various members of the Chromatics (formerly the OK Chorale) of Greenbelt, Maryland, 1994-95, for sing-testing all these arrangements - sometimes many, many times - and providing valuable feedback in the form of comments, suggestions, and the occasional evocative facial expression. They were, alphabetically: Padi Boyd, Charles Brown, T. J. Ciaffone, Tom Foote, Deb Nixon, John Hagedorn, William Hartung, Lisa Kelleher, Paul Kolb, Steve Leete, Linda Markush, Ian Richardson, Beth Riggs, Angela Russo, Alan Smale and Holly Thomas.

In addition, Deke would like to thank Katy Sharon for her love, patience and willingness to plumb the lower limits of the female voice in search of the perfect alto line; and Anne would like to thank Bob Chilcott, whose own arrangements and enthusiasm for the a cappella form proved an irresistible lure into the world of voice-leading and chord inversions.

Good Old Acapella

Arrangement by
Deke Sharon and Anne Raugh

Words and Music by
L. Carter and O.Nevada

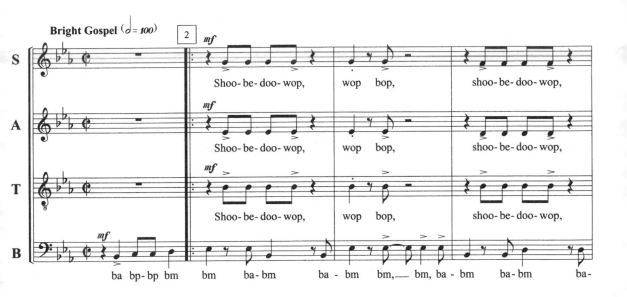

shoo - be - doo - wop, There's a light____ that's from my win -

shoo - be - doo - wop, hoo hoo hoo. oo

shoo - be - doo - wop, hoo hoo hoo. oo

shoo - be - doo - wop, ba - ba - ba hoo hoo hoo, ba bp - bp bm bm ba - bm ba -

— dow,____ and it shines down on the street.____ There's some guys stand-ing on the cor -

oo____ oo,____

oo____ oo,____

bm bm,__ bm, ba - bm ba - bm ba - bm bm__ ba - ba - bm ba - bm ba -

— ner, They're mak-ing some good old__ har - mo - ny.__ Now, this light that's from my win -

good old__ har - mo - ny.__ hoo oo__

good old__ har - mo - ny.__ hoo oo__

bm bm__ ba - bm good old__ har - mo - ny.__ ba bp - bp bm bm ba - bm ba -

dow sets the stage for the street cor-ner sym-pho-ny.___ Let it___ shine, let them___

oo - oo - oo___ oo___

oo - oo - oo___ oo___

bm bm,___ bm, ba-bm ba-bm ba-bm bm___ ba-ba-bm ba-bm ba-

sing, and make that good old___ har-mo-ny.___ Sing-ing___ soul to soul,___

good old___ har-mo-ny.___ soul to soul,___

good old___ har-mo-ny.___ soul to soul,___

bm bm___ ba-bm good old___ har-mo-ny.___ soul to soul,___

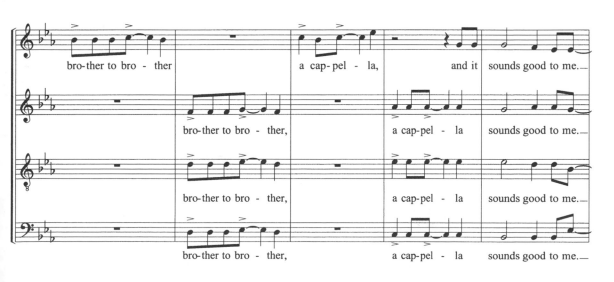

bro-ther to bro - ther a cap-pel - la, and it sounds good to me.

bro-ther to bro - ther, a cap-pel - la sounds good to me.

bro-ther to bro - ther, a cap-pel - la sounds good to me.

bro-ther to bro - ther, a cap-pel - la sounds good to me.

Good old— —There's a sound in the neigh-bor-hood,— and it's

— — hoo oo——— oo - oo -

— — hoo oo——— oo - oo -

— ba bp-bp bm bm ba-bm ba-bm bm,— bm, ba-

sound ing— might y good.— There's some guys stand-ing un-der the light,— And they're

oo——— oo - oo - oo,———

oo——— oo - oo - oo,———

bm ba-bm ba - bm bm— ba-ba bm ba-bm ba-bm bm— ba-bm

sing-ing a-gain— to-night.— Sing-ing that good old— a cap-pel - la, That

sing-ing a-gain— to-night. hoo oo——— oo - oo -

sing-ing a-gain— to-night,— hoo oo——— oo - oo -

sing-ing a-gain— to-night.— ba bp-bp bm bm ba-bm ba-bm bm,— bm, ba-

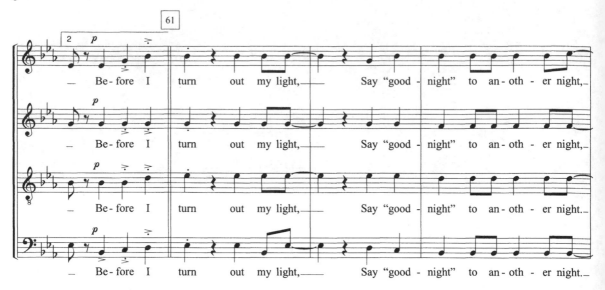

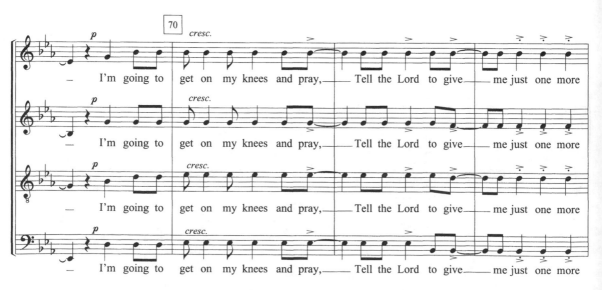

day, "Oh— Lord,— hear my plea,— That mu-sic means so much— to
day, "Oh— Lord,— hear my plea,— mu-sic means so much to
day, "Oh— Lord,— hear my plea,— mu-sic means so much to
day, "Oh— Lord,— hear my plea,— mu-sic means so much to

78

me." And I'm sing-ing— soul to soul,— and bro-ther to bro-ther,
me." oo, soul to soul,— oo,
me." oo, soul to soul,— oo,
me." oo, soul to soul,— oo,

a cap-pel - la, and it sounds good to me.—
bro-ther to bro - ther, oo a cap-pel - la sounds good to me,
bro-ther to bro - ther, oo a cap-pel - la sounds good to me,
bro-ther to bro - ther, oo a cap-pel - la sounds good to me,

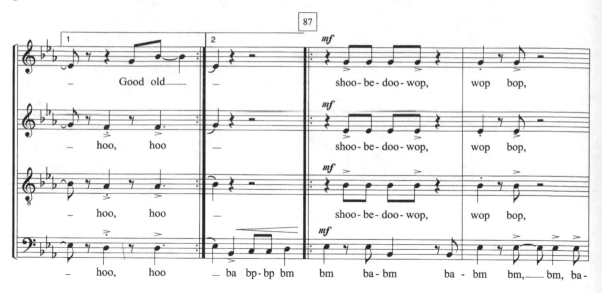

Under the Boardwalk

Arrangement by
Deke Sharon and Anne Raugh

Words and Music by
Artie Resnick and Kenny Young

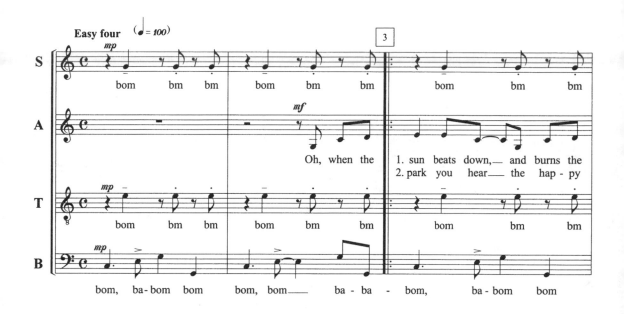

10

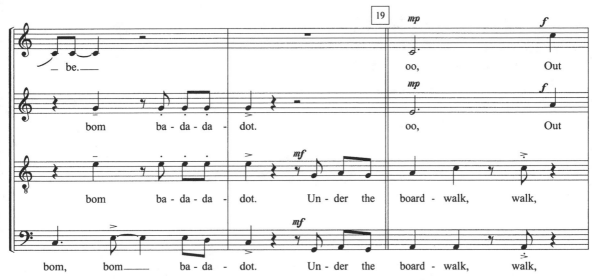

In the Still of the Nite
(I'll Remember)

Arrangement by
Deke Sharon and Anne Raugh

Words and music by
Fred Parros

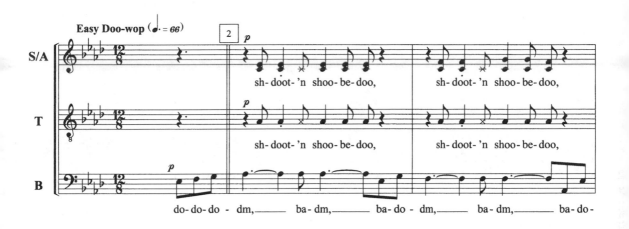

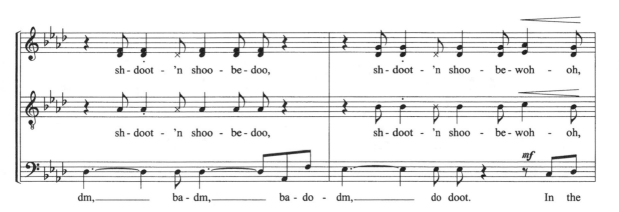

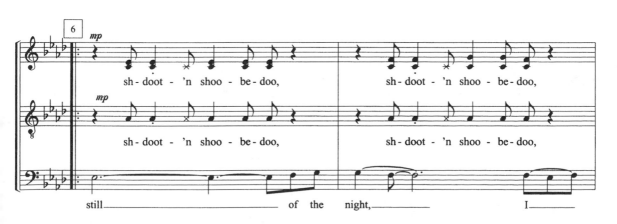

14

Only You

Arrangement by
Deke Sharon and Anne Raugh

Words and Music by
Vince Clarke

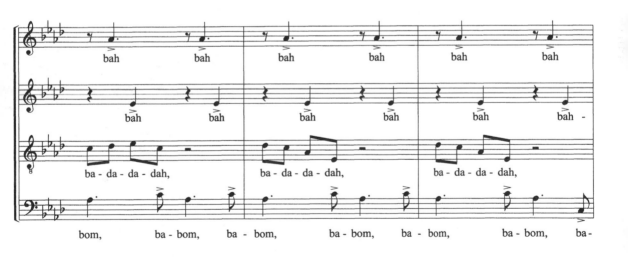

18

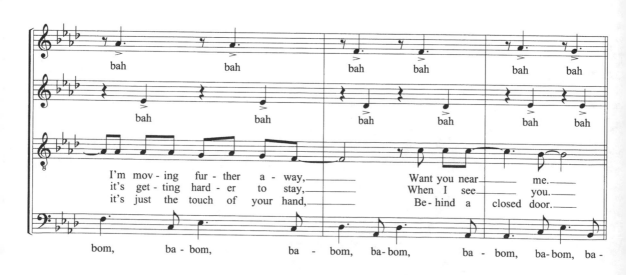

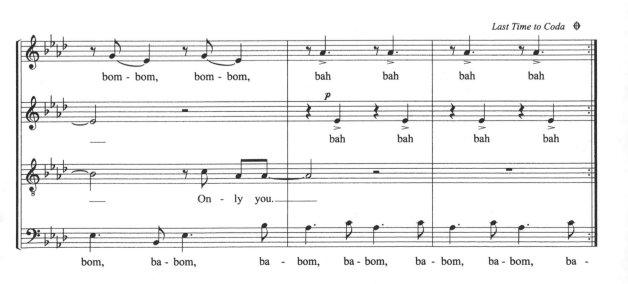

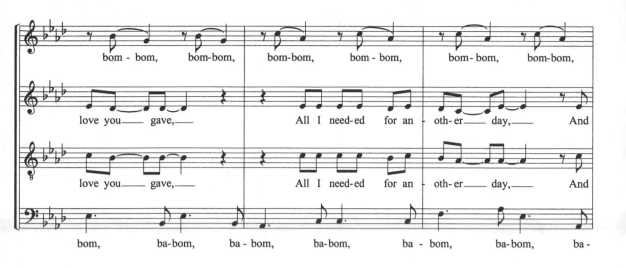

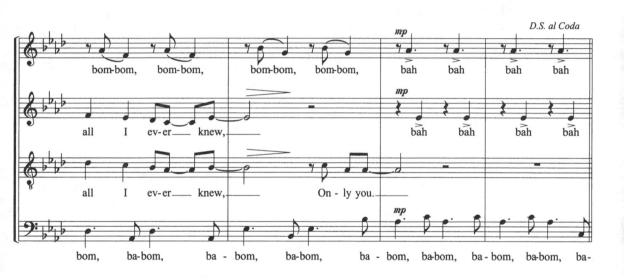

Zombie Jamboree
(Back to Back)

Arrangement by
Deke Sharon and Anne Raugh

Words and Music by
Conrad Eugene Mauge, Jr.

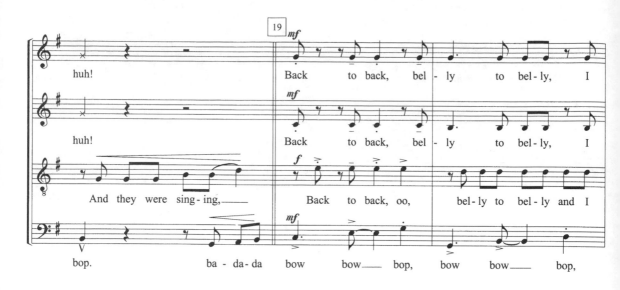

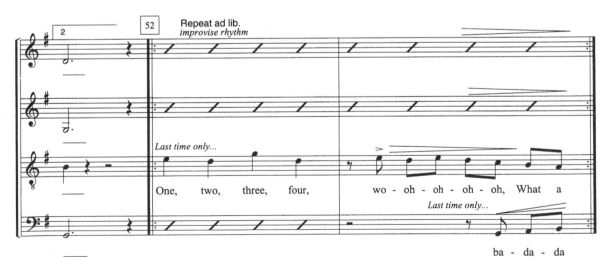

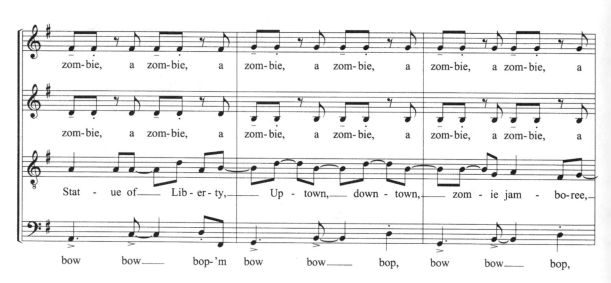

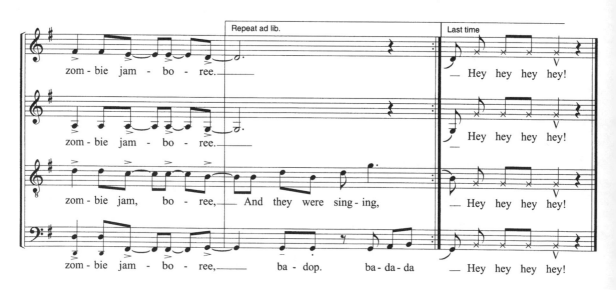

Silhouettes

Arrangement by
Deke Sharon and Anne Raugh

By
Frank C. Slay, Jr. and Bob Crewe

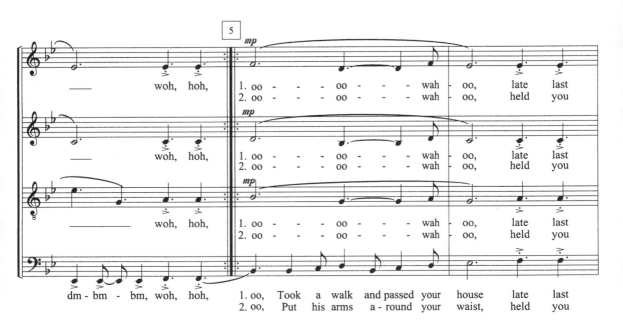

Longest Time

Arrangement by
Deke Sharon and Anne Raugh

Words and Music by
Billy Joel

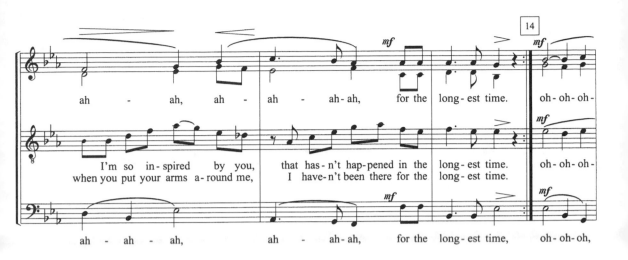

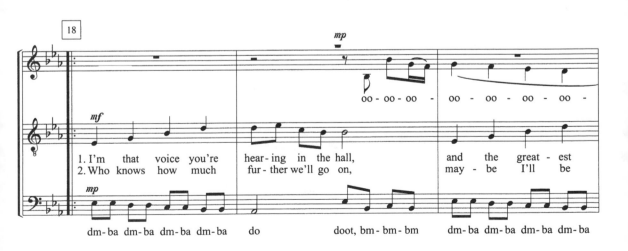

38

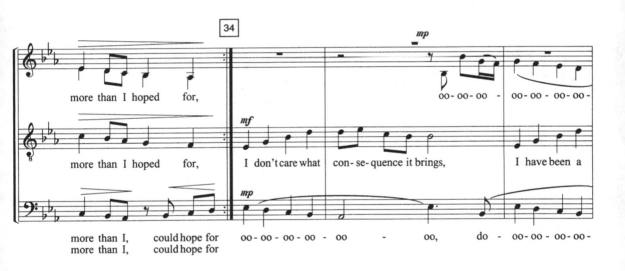

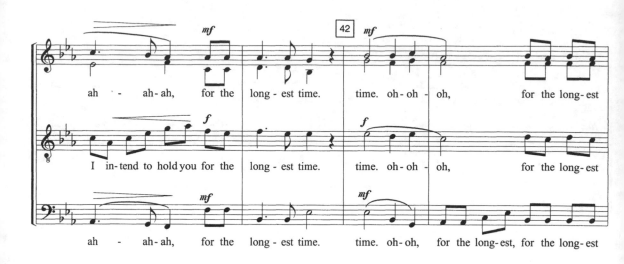

Up on the Roof

Arrangement by
Deke Sharon and Anne Raugh

Words and Music by
Gerry Goffin and Carole King

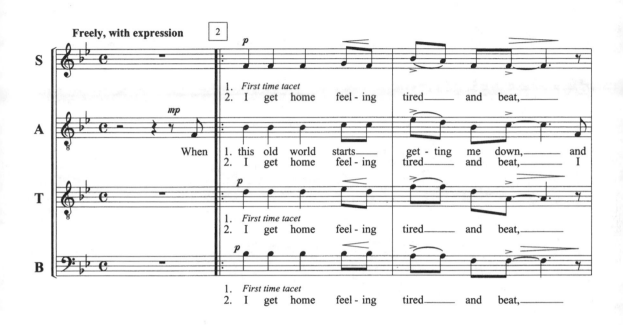

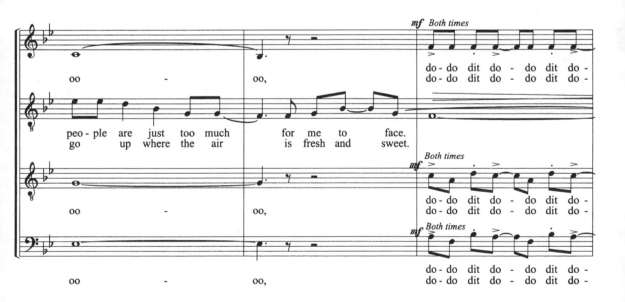

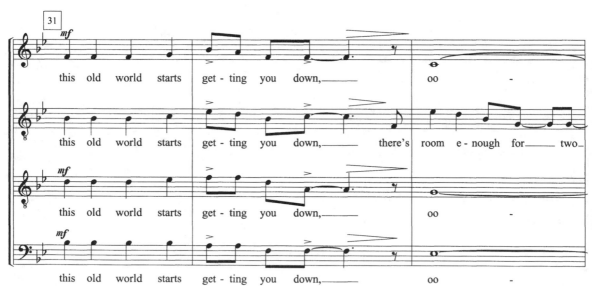

Na Na Hey Hey Kiss Him Goodbye

Arrangement by
Deke Sharon and Anne Raugh

Words and Music by
Gary DeCarlo, Paul Leka and Dale Frashuer

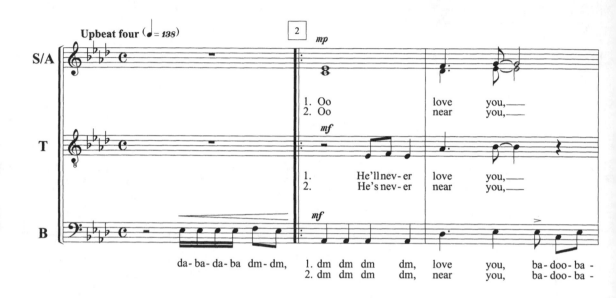

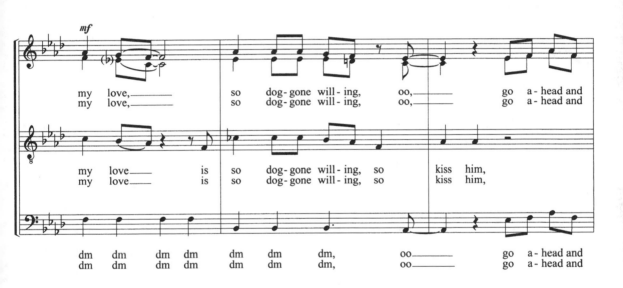

bye. Na - na na - na, na - na - na - na, hey hey hey, good - bye.

Na Na - na na - na, na - na - na - na, hey hey hey, good - bye.

bye. Na - na na - na, na - na - na - na, hey hey hey, good - bye. dm - ba - dm - ba

kiss him, kiss him, oo kiss him, oo

go a-head and kiss him, oo go a-head and kiss him, oo go on and

dm dm dm dm, kiss him, dm ba doo dm dm dm, kiss him, dm ba-doo dm dm dm,

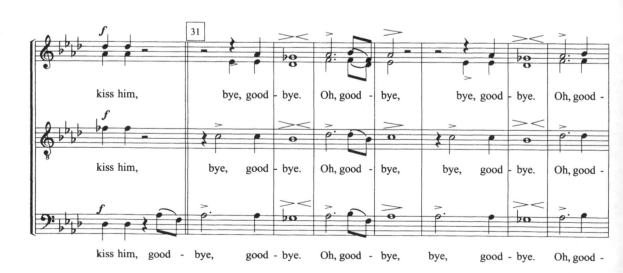

kiss him, bye, good - bye. Oh, good - bye, bye, good - bye. Oh, good -

kiss him, bye, good - bye. Oh, good - bye, bye, good - bye. Oh, good -

kiss him, good - bye, good - bye. Oh, good - bye, bye, good - bye. Oh, good -

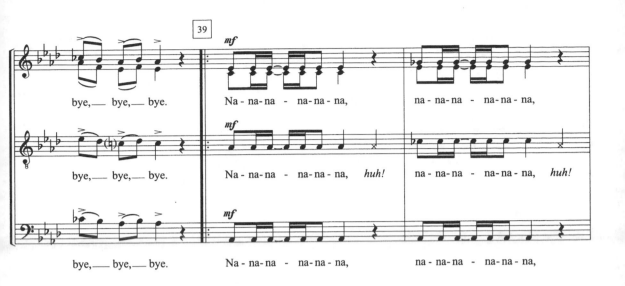

Goodnight, Sweetheart, Goodnight

Arrangement by
Deke Sharon and Anne Raugh

By
Calvin Carter and James Hudson

52

10

54

Good-night, Sweet-heart, well,—it's time to go.—— I hate to leave you but I

Good-night, Sweet-heart, well,—it's time to go.—— I hate to leave you but I

Good-night, Sweet-heart, well,—it's time to go.—— I hate to leave you but I

bom——— ba dm——ba dm bm. ba-da-da-da-da-dm, dm ba-dm, dm ba-

2nd time ritard.

real - ly must say,————— Good - night, Sweet - heart, good - night,

real - ly must say,————— Good - night, Sweet - heart, good - night,

real - ly must say,————— Good - night, Sweet - heart, good - night,

dm, dm ba-dm, bm, Good - night, Sweet - heart, good - night,

1.

good - night.—— Now,——

good - night.—— Now,——

good - night.—— Now,——

— good - night.—— Now,——

2.

night. Good - night.——

night. Good - night.——

night. Good - night.——

your night. Good - night.——

DISCOGRAPHY

Most of the songs in this songbook appear in many recordings. Listed here are recordings which are either *a cappella*, or definitive. Most can be ordered from your local record store or from the *Primarily A Cappella* catalog (call 800-827-2936). Non-*a cappella* recordings are marked with an asterisk (*).

Good Old Acapella

The Nylons, *Four on the Floor* [1], 1991. Attic 72392 75224-2.
Acappella, *Gold*, 1994. Acappella Company-Word 701 9454 607.
The Trenchcoats, *It Turns Me On*, 1992.

Goodnight, Sweetheart, Goodnight

* The Spaniels, *The Doo-Wop Hall of Fame Vol. 1*, 1994. Juke Box
    Treasures 6016.
* The Spaniels, *The Doo-Wop Box*, 1993. Rhino R2 71463.
  "Everyone", *Harmony Sweepstakes National A Cappella Festival
    1996*, 1996. Primarily A Cappella PAC2596.

In the Still of the Nite

Boyz II Men, *The Jacksons: an American Dream Soundtrack*,
    1993.
Boyz II Men, *Cooley High Harmony*, 1993. Motown 314-530231-2.
* The Five Satins, *The Doo-Wop Box*, 1993. Rhino R2 71463.

The Longest Time

* Billy Joel, *An Innocent Man*, 1983. CBS Records CK 38837.

Na Na Hey Hey Kiss Him Goodbye

The Nylons, *Happy Together*, 1987. Open Air OD-0306.
The Nylons, *Four on the Floor* [1], 1991. Attic 72392 75224-2.
The Belmonts, *Cigars, Acappela, Candy*, 1990. Elektra 60989-2.

Only You

The Flying Pickets, *Lost Boys*, 1987. Moving Target MTD 021.
The Flying Pickets, *The Best of...*, 1991. Virgin VVIPD 111.
The Flying Pickets, *The Original Flying Pickets Vol. 1*, 1994. East
    West 4509-98245-2.
The Flying Pickets, *Modern A Cappella* [2], 1992. Rhino R2 71083,
    OPCD-1623.
* Yaz, *Upstairs at Eric's*, 1982. Sire 9 23737-2.

Silhouettes

The Nylons, *One Size Fits All*, 1982. Open Air OD-0301 DIDX 187.
The Nylons, *Modern A Cappella* [2], 1992. Rhino R2 71083, OPCD-1623.

Under the Boardwalk

Rockapella and True Image, *Spike & Co.: Do It A Cappella* [2], 1990. Elektra 9 60953-2.
The Persuasions, *No Frills*, 1986. Rounder CD 3083.
The Edlos, *Meet Me in the Lobby*, 1992. Auriga AURCD-1992-1.
The Diners, *Open All Night*, 1992. Blue Plate BPCD-01.

Up on the Roof

The Persuasions, *Acapella*, 1989. Enigma Retro-Straight 7 73396-2.
The Persuasions, *Spike & Co.: Do It A Cappella* [2], 1990. Elektra 9 60953-2.
The Nylons, *The Nylons*, 1982. Attic ACD 1125.
The Nylons, *Seamless*, 1986. Open Air OD-0304.
The Nylons, *Four on the Floor* [1], 1991. Attic 72392 75224-2.
Vito & The Twilights, *Starlight Serenade Vol. 5*. SCD 19931.

Zombie Jamboree

Rockapella, *Two: From NY*, 1992. For Life FLCF-30137.
Rockapella, *Spike & Co.: Do It A Cappella* [2], 1990. Elektra 9 60953-2.
Rockapella, *Modern A Cappella* [2], 1992. Rhino R2 71083, OPCD-1623.
* The Kingston Trio, *The Kingston Trio/The Kingston Trio—...from the "Hungry i"*, 1992. Capitol CDP 7 96748 2.

1 Live recording
2 Compilation album

PERFORMANCE NOTES

Every arrangement in this book is a distillation of the best known elements of some of the most frequently performed *a cappella* cover songs. Each is intended to be accessible to singers of all ages and abilities. If you're singing with a more experienced group, feel free to elaborate, experiment and improvise on these arrangements to make them your own. This is easiest when you have only one singer on a voice part; sectional improvisation requires some structure when dealing with a chorus. You can "loosen up" the solo or bass part, add a fifth part to make every chord a close-voiced triad, or you can add some vocal percussion - the sky's the limit.

Included below are suggestions for adapting the arrangements for use by TTBB and SSAA groups. The translation to TTBB is usually the most direct. In SSAA adaptations, bear in mind that the contemporary *a cappella* style makes heavy use of the female chest register in both altos and sopranos, and be prepared to shift parts of lines up an octave when the range temporarily drops below that of the low alto chest voice, returning when range permits. Finally, remember that each *a cappella* group is unique, so don't hesitate to experiment with the voices to find the adaptation that works best for you.

[Note that tenor-only lines are notated in treble clef (as for soprano and alto) but transposed up an octave from where they actually sound, as indicated by the small number "8" under the clef sign. This transposed clef is also used for the alto solo line in "Up on the Roof".]

Good Old Acapella: The background in this song must be kept light under the verses to avoid overwhelming the lead, but should match the lead in volume during the call-and-answer chorus. When a solo voice has the lead, the melody can be taken very freely. Snapping on 2 and 4 can help propel the song along and provide a backbeat, but be careful of rushing. This song has been used by many *a cappella* groups to open their show, and several have written their own fourth verse to introduce the group.

> **TTBB**: TI sing the alto line at pitch; TII sings the soprano line down an octave; BI and BII sing the tenor and bass lines, respectively.

> **SSAA**: SI sings the tenor line up an octave; SII takes the soprano line; AI sings the alto line; AII takes the bass line, up an octave. You may want to transpose the entire arrangement down to C major or lower once you've learned it.

Under the Boardwalk: There should be just the slightest hint of a calypso feel during the verses. Vocal percussion by one or more singers might be fun - imagine a *t-t-k-t-t-k-t-k* pattern of eighths each measure, where "*t*" is a high-hat and "*k*" is a snare drum sound. The crescendo in the last three measures should be as dramatic as possible to close the tune decisively.

> **TTBB**: Sing as written, substituting TTBB for SATB. TI should either drop an octave when singing melody lines in the high C-D area or take them in falsetto.

> **SSAA**: SI takes soprano; SII alto; AI sings the tenor part at pitch (i.e., an octave below where it's written); AII takes the bass line at pitch where it lies at low C and above, lower pitches are transposed up one octave. Note that this will eliminate some octave leaps, but the notes should be repeated at pitch to maintain the rhythm. The AII singer(s) must be careful to maintain full chest resonance to distinguish the part from the very close tenor line.

In the Still of the Nite: If you have five or more voices, consider continuing the bass line throughout the song and having a separate soloist (male or female). Watch the *bom*s in measure 23 - they should have a triplet feel and be smooth, not overly syncopated. Some sort of variation can be introduced the second time through the repeat which starts at measure 6, since the verse is the same. Using a continuous *oo* rather than the written syllables, for example, produces a softer feel. Alternately, try repeating back to the bridge at measure 16 rather than the verse at measure 6. This song is so well known that the Persuasions use it in concert as a sing-along, inviting members of the audience on stage to join in.

TTBB: As written.

SSAA: Also as written, with AI taking the tenor line at pitch and AII taking the bass line up an octave.

Only You: Treat this tune gently. The opening figure between bass, soprano and alto must be carefully balanced to give the feeling of an arpeggio being played on guitar or piano. Note also that these background *bah*s should sound like bell tones, i.e., there is a slight accent on the "b", but the vowel is held out. Tenors and altos not used to singing sustained tones low in their respective registers should also be mindful of matching vowel sounds in measures 23-26.

TTBB: As is; TI should drop an octave for the instrumental section at measure 23.

SSAA: Transpose the entire arrangement up a major third to C (or to comfort) and take all parts at the new pitch, SI taking soprano, SII alto, AI tenor and AII bass.

Zombie Jamboree: The ad lib. rhythm sections provide a good opportunity to play with the audience a bit, introduce members of the group, or show of your vocal percussionist (listen to the Rockapella version to get a sense of the intro). Note the unusually wide spacing between soprano and alto which gives this arrangement its distinctive flavor. If you have a fifth voice, add a third part to complete these triads. When singing this low in chest register, altos should take care to match vowels with the sopranos so these intervals can ring the way they should.

TTBB: As is. If the tenor solo line is too high for BI, switch it with the TII (alto) line.

SSAA: SI takes the tenor melody up an octave; SII takes the soprano line; AI the alto; AII the bass line up one octave.

Silhouettes: The repeat in the first four bars is optional; it should probably not be sung more than twice unless it's being used as a background for group introductions, song set-up, or to cover some other activity. In the echo sections (starting at measures 14 and 27), notice that while the alto always enters on beats 2 and 4 and the tenor on 1 and 3, the soprano and bass switch their entrances in the second measure. At measure 19, the background *dit-dit-dit* triplet figure must be kept very light to avoid obscuring the lyrics in the bass.

TTBB: As is. If you have a fifth voice, continue the bass line through the verse.

SSAA: SI sings the tenor line up an octave; SII takes soprano; AI alto; AII takes the bass line up an octave.

Longest Time: Nearly every measure of this contemporary favorite is repeated at least once. Consequently, special attention should be paid to blend, phrasing and dynamics in order to keep it fresh and exciting throughout. If you have a chorus, try different tenor soloists on each verse or section. Snap on 2 and 4 to maintain the back beat and give a streetcorner feel.

TTBB: As written. If your singers are versatile enough, switch TI, TII and BI around during the song so that each has the solo line at some point.

SSAA: SI takes the soprano line; SII the alto; AI the tenor line at pitch and AII the bass line up one octave, adding an additional octave where needed on the lowest notes. The entire arrangement may be more comfortable if taken up a note or two, depending on the ranges in your group.

Up on the Roof: This arrangement is a more dramatic setting than most in this book and requires subtlety and attention to dynamics. Note that the lead in the alto line is notated using the tenor clef and should be sung one octave down from the written pitch. When the lead is carried by a single voice it can be taken rubato throughout while the background figures remain precise. Here *doo* has been abbreviated to *do* in the interests of spacing.

> **TTBB**: As is.

> **SSAA**: This is one of the few arrangements in the world that can be sung almost entirely as is by men or women, although you may prefer to raise it a step or two for comfort. The lowest notes in the bass line on the last page will most likely need to be transposed up an octave even when the entire arrangement is taken up.

Na Na Hey Hey Kiss Him Goodbye: After your group becomes comfortable with this arrangement they will probably want to do something more rhythmically interesting under the verses beginning in measure 2. This would be a good place to try some vocal percussion. Alternately, in a quartet the bass can be set free to improvise a more interesting pattern around the chord(s) in each measure. Note that the "b" of "bye" should be slightly accented to produce the bell tone effect on the building chord in measure 31. Beginning with the start of the tenor solo in measure 44, there should be a gradual build driving toward the end of the song; tenors should feel free to improvise from here until the final measure. You can start the song with a rubato section (as in the Nylons' version), or with an audible count ("One, two, three...").

> **TTBB**: As is.

> **SSAA**: Besides probably changing the lyric to "kiss *her* goodbye," this can be sung mostly as is, but the second alto will need to take the lower bass notes up an octave. You'll probably want to take this up a step or two, as all four voices will be in their lowest register.

Goodnight, Sweetheart, Goodnight: Note that, although the tenors have the lead in the first chorus and all verses, the sopranos have the lead in the remaining choruses. Volume levels must be adjusted accordingly. This is a good audience sing-along number and a great way to close a show that has featured a number of *a cappella* groups (bring them all out on stage together). This arrangement is dedicated to Lisa Murphy, founder of the *Harmony Sweepstakes*, a national a cappella competition which has adopted this song as its theme.

> **TTBB**: As is. You'll need to have the melody in the chorus section falsetto unless you have a screamin' tenor.

> **SSAA**: As is, but with the bass line up an octave. If Al is having trouble with the low range of the tenor line, either take the line up an octave or switch the solo among the upper three voices.

The folks at CASA are always ready to help with any aspect of *a cappella*. Have a performance question? Give 'em a call: (415) 563-5224 (California, USA).

WHAT IS CASA?

The Contemporary A Cappella Society of America
is a non-profit organization formed in 1990 to foster and promote a cappella music. Our members include thousands of fans and vocalists as well as professional, collegiate, and recreational a cappella groups around the world.

For only $15 a year, as a Basic Member, you'll receive:

THE CONTEMPORARY A CAPPELLA NEWS (the **CAN**) is bi-monthly and includes:
> CURRENT NEWS about what's going on in *a cappella* everywhere.
> CALENDAR of upcoming *a cappella* concerts and events around the world.
> CONCERT REVIEWS of performances by your favorite groups.
> INTERVIEWS with top groups (Take 6, the Nylons, the King's Singers, etc.).
> ALBUM REVIEWS of new releases by professional and collegiate groups.
> HOW-TO ARTICLES ranging from starting groups to recording techniques.
> ADVERTISING including classifieds for new albums, groups looking for members and gig opportunities.

If you're in a group or serious about *a cappella*, you'll want an Advanced Membership. For $30 a year, you'll get our newsletter (and one free classified in it) plus:

THE *A CAPPELLA* YELLOW PAGES: the definitive directory of professional, collegiate and recreational groups, plus important contacts and *a cappella*-affiliated organizations around the world.

ADDITIONAL DISCOUNTS on *a cappella*-related merchandise and services, including custom arrangements with the Ultimate A Cappella Arranging Service, recordings, songbooks and album manufacturing.

Note: Each group member (after the first) can get his own copy of the newletter for only $10 a year.

OTHER CASA PROGRAMS

THE URBAN HARMONY MOVEMENT brings *a cappella* concerts to inner-city public schools and helps schools get groups started. Our unique program combines currently popular repertoire in sheet music and parts tapes, taught by trained volunteers.

TELEPHONE CONSULTATION AND HELP is available every day. We offer experience and advice on every aspect of *a cappella*, including: performing; producing an album; singing full-time; helping individuals looking to start or join a group; and getting local community members in touch with groups in their area.

CASA AMBASSADORS are volunteers spread across five continents who serve local members and groups in many ways, from finding information to keeping you aware of local shows or helping you put on your own.

OTHER SERVICES include: the Contemporary *A Cappella* Recording Awards, the *a cappella* recording archives, the National Championship of College *A Cappella*, *A Cappella* Radio International, and the semi-annual international *A Cappella* Summit. We produce *a cappella*-related materials, including informative booklets like "The Definitive *A Cappella* Press Kit," and compilation albums such as the "Best of College *A Cappella*" CDs.

If you're interested in helping CASA grow, you can become a Sponsor with a tax deductible donation of $50 or more (all but $30 is deductible). You'll get a free *a cappella* album and other special offers as well as all the benefits above, and you'll help us fund many of the programs we offer.

TO JOIN CASA send $15 for a basic membership, $30 for advanced membership (plus $10 for each additional group member wanting the CAN), or $50+ to be a sponsor. If you're outside the US, please send an additional $5 to help us cover postage costs. Send check or money order to:

CASA
1850 Union Street, Suite 1441
San Francisco, CA, USA, 94123

For more information, drop us a line:

Phone: (415) 563-5224
Fax: (415) 921-2834
Email: casa@casa.org
World Wide Web: http://www.casa.org/

Other *A Cappella* Resources

Mainly A CAPPELLA CATALOG (MAC)
MAC is a mail-order catalog published annually with quarterly updates. It features hundreds of titles, including rare and international releases. The catalog represents a wide range of styles, from the latest in pop, jazz and world bands to classical ensembles and barbershop harmonies.

NATIONAL CHAMPIONSHIP OF COLLEGE A CAPPELLA (NCCA)
The NCCA hosts numerous competitions that bring together the best from among the hundreds of college *a cappella* groups around the U.S. Winners of regional competitions have traditionally met for an exciting final at venues such as Carnegie Hall and Lincoln Center in New Your. In addition to the competitions themselves, NCCA produces the "Best of Collegiate A Cappella" CDs in collaboration with CASA.

ON-LINE COMMUNITY
The Mainly A CAPPELLA catalog has a popular home page on the World Wide Web, at "www.a–cappella.com". There are hundreds of RealAudio® sound clips to hear, an extensive and continually updated Tour page, and secure on-line buying. There is also a very active newsgroup on the Internet designed exclusively for *a cappella* fans: "rec.music.a–cappella".

Mainly A CAPPELLA and the National Championship
of College A Cappella may be reached at:

PO Box 159
Southwest Harbor, ME 04679
Phone: (800) 827-2936
International: (207) 244-7603
Fax: (207) 244-7613
Email: catalog-request@a-cappella.com
World Wide Web: www.a-cappella.com

For A Free Catalog Call: (800) 827-2936